The Argument
Poems of The Black Experience
in The Workplace

Franklin D. Lewis

The Argument
Poems of The Black Experience in The Workplace

by

Franklin Delano Lewis

DORRANCE PUBLISHING CO., INC.
PITTSBURGH, PENNSYLVANIA 15222

ISBN: 978-1-4349-0125-5
Library of Congress Control Number: 2008926324

Printed in the United States of America

First Printing

For more information or to order additional books, please contact:
Dorrance Publishing Co., Inc.
701 Smithfield Street
Third Floor
Pittsburgh, Pennsylvania 15222
U.S.A.
1-800-788-7654
www.dorrancebookstore.com

Dedication

JOE BUGESS
PHIL CHATHAM
DOUG GATES

Colleagues. Mentors. Friends.

Franklin Delano Lewis

Born in Antigua, West Indies, Franklin D. Lewis came to the United States in 1966 following a six-year residence in England.

After earning a B.A. degree from Hampton Institute (now Hampton University) and an M.A. degree from New York University's Graduate School of Arts and Science, Lewis joined corporate America as an employee relations assistant in 1971. He then progressed through various management levels in human resources with some of America's major corporations.

Now retired, Lewis reflects on his experiences and observations to which his various positions and professional affiliations had exposed him. Affirmative action then, and still often today, incited multiple reactions from different races and employment levels, and Franklin D. Lewis captures several of these in this collection of poems.

Contents

The First Black 1

First Encounters 2

Supervisor's Lament...3

Lip Service 4

The Decision Maker 5

The Resistant Industry 6

Taking Advantage 8

Short Memory...9

Assumption...10

The Affirmative Action Manager Speaks...........................12

A Co-Worker 13

Pressure 14

Upgrade-Downgrade Blues 15

Inconsistency..17

Telephone Acquaintance 18

Father's Send-Off 19

Mother's Send-Off 20

Ripples..21

The Invisible Activists 24

Chance Meeting 25

The Argument...28

All by Themselves 35

Preface

In 1961, President John F. Kennedy created the Committee on Equal Employment Opportunity, and issued Executive Order 10925 which introduced the term "affirmative action" in referring to programs designed to achieve non-discrimination. President Lyndon B. Johnson issued Executive Order 11246 in 1965 requiring every federal government contractor and subcontractor with at least fifty employees to develop and implement an affirmative action plan to correct underutilization of specific minority groups. This was amended in 1968 to include females. One of the minority groups was blacks (the term African Americans had not yet come into usage).

The resulting increase in employment of black employees in nontraditional positions created new encounters, attitudes, understandings, and misunderstandings for the incoming and receiving workforces. The introduction of the 1965 executive order sparked a decades-long attack on, and defense of, affirmative action, which although never dead, has found new life in the 2000s.

It was during the early years of affirmative action that Franklin D. Lewis entered the workforce to spend a career in human resources management. His various positions have enabled him to experience, observe, and hear the situations he has captured in these poems of the black experience in the workforce. Some of these were first published in Hampton University's *Journal of Ethnic Studies,* but most have been unpublished until now. In the title poem, *The Argument,* he presents his own argument for affirmative action. In the closing poem, *All By Themselves,* Lewis contends that affirmative action has been so successful, it has created a new enemy—the successful black executive.

The First Black

He was the first; the only black till then
To reach his level in that company.
And so he'd flaunt it, time and time again,
How prominent his rise had made him be.
Until one day, reflection made him pause,
And he was angered so much that he cursed
To think that he had glorified the cause
Why in these times he still could be a first.
He realized prestige had come his way
Through previous opportunities denied.
And those before who'd all been turned away
Weren't necessarily less qualified.
Now he no longer cares for fame to win,
But strives instead to get his brothers in.

First Encounters

I wonder how their necks don't break
With a resounding crack,
When they perform that double take
On seeing that I'm black.

Supervisor's Lament

Now there are two of them,
And I've got a crisis on my hands.
You'd expect those guys in Personnel
Would think twice
Before placing
Two blacks in one department.
Now I've got two,
While some departments have none.
So I've got to spend my time
Watching them,
When I've got a department to run.
There's no telling
What they can get up to together.
They arrive at work together,
And leave together.
They even sit together in the lunchroom.
They're always together.
Always.
Together.
What can they be up to?
They put two blacks in my department,
And I've got a crisis on my hands.

Lip Service

How can the company be so ungrateful
To one who's proved to be so faithful?
When they announced we'd hire on merit,
Didn't I say that I was for it?
And when they said that things like color,
Religion, age, and sex won't matter
In deciding who'd be hired,
Promoted, transferred, laid off, fired,
Didn't I say that this was fine,
And declare loudly, "It's about time!"
Didn't I speak of rights and justice,
And how progressive a decision this is?
Wasn't I the one who expounded
On the tenets on which our country's founded?
Then how is it that I'm the one
The company has so undone
By forcing me, as my allotment,
To hire minorities in my department?

The Decision Maker

Despite their high requirements,
His credentials and accomplishments
Fit to a tee.
His manner was the very best,
And they all thought that he was dressed
Impeccably.

And this group of senior management
Evaluating applicants
Was quite impressed.
Of all the candidates they'd seen,
The seasoned and the very green,
He was the best.

But they'd been thorough in this case,
And would not now decide in haste,
And then regret.
Thus, after reconsidering,
They all agreed there was one thing
They had to check.

So the executives summoned forth the lady
Who would be his secretary,
And inquired of her,
"Would you object tremendously
If your new boss turns out to be
A man of color?"

The Resistant Industry

We know our workforce does suggest
Our company's anti-black;
And that's a shame, for the reverse
Is actually the fact
But others in our industry
Don't share our progressive view;
So they're the ones who hold us back
From things we'd like to do.
We'd like to hire all the blacks we can get,
But our industry isn't ready as yet.

Our customers might not understand
Our sending a rep who's black.
They'll think our intention's to offend
And hold their orders back.
And if we lose our clientele
Our business would be through;
So, hiring one would do more harm
Than the little good it'd do.
We'd like to hire all the blacks we can get,
But our industry isn't ready as yet.

A receptionist sits out at the front
In unobstructed view.
How could we put a black out there
With visitors coming through?
For those who call upon our firm
Don't think the same as we;
They're so behind, you'd think they're in
Another century.
We'd like to hire all the blacks we can get,
But our industry isn't ready as yet.

To give a black a foreman's job
Supervising whites,
Is to cause resentment, and even more,
Create a stream of fights.
They'd make that foreman feel the sting
Of their cruel racial jokes.
They'd refuse to whatever he'd say,
And sabotage the works.
We'd like to hire all the blacks we can get,
But our industry isn't ready as yet.

So, now you see we're really not
As bad as we appear,
For, in our unobtrusive way,
We're quite a pioneer.
We've placed blacks in our typing pool,
Our mail room and shop floor,
But, till our industry awakes,
We can't do anymore.
We'd like to hire all the blacks we can get,
But our industry just isn't ready as yet.

Taking Advantage

She sees no need to do her share;
By threats she's not inspired.
Erroneously, she heard somewhere
That blacks are never fired.

Short Memory.

I've intervened for you before,
Two or three times, maybe more.
And once, I even saved the day
When they tried to take your job away.
But when I thought that you were wrong,
And urged you to be less headstrong,
You said it seems that my position
Gives me a haughty disposition.
You claimed I think that I'm much better
Than all you other blacks together.
I disagree, but am aware
You don't expect me to be fair.
You think I should be anti-white,
And though you're wrong, still say you're right.
Now I won't let this bother me,
Or lose my objectivity;
But the thing that has me so upset,
Is to learn how quickly you forget.

Assumption

To Fred Adair the world looked good, his heart was feeling light,
For he was sure beyond a doubt that things were going right.
This day he'd lay the groundwork that would land a big account,
And his commission from the deal would be a large amount.

He'd written to the target firm for well nigh on three years,
And telephoned to no avail, and oft was close to tears.
Till finally, Jack Abington, the head of Purchasing,
Because of his persistence, agreed to meet with him.

And so he called upon the firm at the appointed hour
To try to overwhelm a man he'd never met before.
And in the lobby, he announced to the receptionist seated there,
"Jack Abington's expecting me. My name is Fred Adair."

She smiled and said, "Please have a seat." And then she made a call
To let Jack know that Fred Adair was waiting in the hall.
On hanging up, she said, "He'll be here any moment now.
He'll bring his new assistant too, a buyer named Phil Howe."

So there Fred was awaiting Jack; his chance had come at last
To gain the big account he'd yearned and chased these three years past.
He mustn't seem excited now; he must be poised and cool,
And utilize the selling ploys he'd learned in training school.

Soon, just beyond an inner door, two men came into sight.
The door was glass, so he could see one man was black, one white.
And since the door was only built for access one-by-one,
The black man was the first one through; the other followed on.

On seeing both, Fred guessed at once Jack was the one behind.
Surely, he had to be the boss; and with this thought in mind,
Walked past the first, approached the next, offered his hand, and said,
"Good morning, Mr. Abington. We meet at last. I'm Fred."

What happened next took Frederick's breath and stopped him in mid-stride;
For he to whom he gave his hand, ignored it, and replied,
"I'm afraid that you're mistaken, sir, for I am Phillip Howe,
And that was Mr. Abington you walked right by just now."

And later, in the washroom, as Phil stood near to Fred,
The salesman, with a humble air, to the buyer turned and said,"
I wish I'd known before I came exactly who was who.
I just assumed that you were Jack, and thought that he was you."

But the sympathy expected was in short supply that day,
For Phil, in his response to Fred, had only this to say,
"I've often heard it said before, but now I clearly see,
Whenever you **ASSUME**, you make an **ASS** of **U** and **ME**."

The Affirmative Action Manager Speaks

Now, I'm not fooled for one minute.
I know exactly why I was hired
As Affirmative Action Manager.
My responsibility
Is to keep this company
Out of trouble.
I'm expected to protect it
From the EEOC,
And OFCCP,
And state and local
Human Rights agencies.
I must not risk losing
Our federal government contracts,
Or sales to other contractors.
I'm in the business of protecting profits,
Not helping people.
And I understand that.
And find no discomfort in it,
For, in achieving the Company's objectives,
I'll achieve some of my own.
Satisfying the compliance agencies
Requires concerted effort
In recruiting,
Training,
And promoting
Those who would be denied opportunities
Otherwise.
And the Company must support me
In these efforts
In order to help itself.
So, I'll protect the profits;
For, companies without profits
Mean workers without jobs.
And there are some workers
I'd like to see
Placed in those jobs.
So I'm willing to form an alliance;
If the Company gives me its support,
I'll defend it to the best of my ability,
And achieve both our goals.

A Co-worker

With crime, elections, movies to see,
And topics of all sorts,
How is it when he speaks to me
He only speaks of sports?

Pressure

Now, who would have thought
Being able to fail
Would get to be such an achievement?
People fail every day,
And their failure
Incites no more reaction
Than the sympathy we feel
For those beset by misfortune.
Then why can't I also fail?
It's not that I'd like to.
In fact, I'd hate to.
But it hurts to know I can't if I wish.
For I'll never permit them to say of me,
"Well, what did you expect?"
Or perhaps, "Blacks want the opportunity,
But can't handle the responsibility."
Or, worst of all,
"That's the last one o' them we'll hire."
So the pressure persists,
And threatens to remain
Until I'm confident
My failure won't be linked to race.
Would you have thought
Being able to fail
Would get to be such an achievement?

Upgrade-Downgrade Blues

My spirit's kinda low today:
Got the Upgrade-Downgrade Blues.
I said my spirit's low today;
Feeling the Upgrade-Downgrade Blues.
Whichever way they grade a job,
It always means I lose.

My boss just upped and quit his job,
And I was next in line.
When my last boss resigned his job,
I thought I was in line,
But they upgraded that job so high,
It was out of reach this time.

The time before, a guy retired
And opened a spot for me.
When that old working man retired,
The way looked clear for me
Till they downgraded that job real low
And killed my opportunity.

Sometimes I see a vacancy
And think I got it made.
Sometimes I see a vacancy
And feel sure I got it made,
But after they manipulate,
I never make the grade.

Sometimes, just to stop me,
They'll roll two jobs in one;
So I get no promotion
When all's said and done.
On other occasions,
They'll split one job in two
So neither half's better than the one I already got,
And there's nothing to move up to...

...that's why I sing these blues.
Now I got nothing left to do
But sing the Upgrade-Downgrade Blues.
Others move on to better jobs,
But I never fill their shoes.

Inconsistency

To get more blacks in corporate spots
Some demonstrate and shout.
And yet, to blacks who take such jobs
They say, "You're selling out."

Telephone Acquaintance

It never did occur to him
that the one to whom he spoke by phone;
a person whom he'd never met
but only telephoned
in the course of his business;
the one to whom he bared his soul,
and confidentially said,
"Just between you and me,
and this telephone,"
and then expressed his prejudices,
uttering every racial epithet
in common use,
even creating some himself;
the one that he assumed empathized with him
in bigotry;
was really black.

Father's Send-Off

Son, dere ain't a whole lot I can say
To help you in yo new job.
An nobody in yo family
Can tell you what to expect.
You see, ain't none o' us
Ever been no executive.
An we don't know nuthin
Bout no corporation job.
You de first, Son.
You de first.
So you got to learn on your own.
Now, dat's a tough row to hoe,
But you's a smart boy, Son,
An I know you goin to make it.
Jus remember,
The Lord give you two eyes an two ears,
But only one mouth.
Dat's so you can see an hear
Twice as much as you say.
An dat's how you learn, Son.
Dat's how you learn.
So you go out dere
An look,
An listen,
An learn fast.
Then you'll be able to hold yo own
Among de best.
For dat's where you belong, Son.
An dat's where you gonna be one day,
Among de best.

Mother's Send-Off

Ooooooooweeeeee
Don't you look nice!
Boy, when you go down to dat company,
Dey goin sit up an take notice o' you.
Jus look at you
Standin dere
In yo brand new three-piece,
Like you goin to church on dis weekday morning.
Yo Daddy ain't never been to work
In no suit before.
But all dat rivetin he did
In dat shipyard,
An all dem days I spen
In dat steamin cafeteria kitchen
To send you to college,
Been worth it just to see you now.
You's de picture o' success.
Yo Daddy's so proud,
He telling everybody
Dey pay him a hourly rate,
But dey have to pay you
In a an-yoo-al salary.
An I'se proud too, Son.
Right proud.
So you jus come here
An give yo Momma some sugar,
Den get yo good lookin self outa here
An go to work.

Ripples

He didn't want the hassle.
So, when the opportunity came
For him to be their first black supervisor,
He turned it down.
And, as a pebble tossed into a pond,
Sinking silently out of sight
In the dark water beneath the surface
Attains oblivion,
So thought he of his refusal.
It, too, would be forgotten;
For, since his decision affected no one else,
No one else would care,
And he would soon forget.

But, as a pebble in its submerged descent
Leaves behind its ripples
As evidence that one below
Had first disturbed the surface,
So too, his decision
Would not be denied its ripples.
Starting only as small circles,
They grew larger as they journeyed outward
In hasty undulation.

And in the north,
The managers felt the ripples,
And said,
"What a shame.
You can't even help some people
To help themselves.
We finally got a hardworking black
With enough experience
To be a leader.
And when we offer to promote him,
He turns us down.
It seems these people
Don't want to use their minds;
They'd rather break their backs instead.
We'd be wasting our time
Developing them to be supervisors.
We'd better concentrate
On those we're sure
Want to move ahead."

And in the west,
The ripples touched his black co-workers,
Who said,
"What a setback.
When our turn comes
To be promoted,
It will be harder to accept
Than if someone had blazed a trail before,
And would be there to advise,
And be a confidant and companion.
Now, the going will be extra tough
For the first of us to be promoted.
How we wish that he'd accepted."

And in the east,
The ripples were effective too;
For there, his white co-workers felt them,
And said,
"What a break.
those blacks don't want
To think for a living;
They only want to sweat.
Now, our competition
Has withdrawn,
And promotion will come to us
More quickly.
How bright the future looks."

And the ripples also flowed to the south,
Bringing the news
To the black junior workers,
Who said dejectedly,
"What a kick in the head.
For once it seemed
We'd have a supervisor
Who'd treat us with dignity,
And listen to our concerns,
And stand up for us
When he knows we're right.
Now, we'll just have to wait,
Not knowing when
Our chance will come again."

And he whose action caused the ripples
Went home and slept contentedly,
As one will do when rid of care.
Unaware was he of his creations—
The pity, anger, hope, despair
Of those whose lives the ripples touched.
He only knew he'd spared himself
The extra work they'd tried to put upon him.
And this meant all to him, because
He didn't want the hassle.

The Invisible Activists

It's all so very confusing.
Minorities claim they contribute
To corporate America's gains
By buying its products.
They think, therefore,
Corporations should employ them,
And purchase from them,
And use their service companies.
They publish directories
Of minority vendors
And minority referral sources.
They advertise,
And demonstrate,
And agitate,
And negotiate.
That's what they claim, and do.
But then comes the source of my confusion.
Despite the advertisements,
And directories,
And publicized rhetoric,
Some company representatives
With assignments to recruit,
And purchase,
And award contracts,
Often return to say,
"In making our decision,
We'd gladly have considered
Any available minority,
But there was none.
We searched.
But couldn't find any."

Couldn't find any?
If they are so visible and vocal
In protesting their underutilization,
Why can't the seekers find them?
I find it so confusing.

Chance Meeting

The cleaning lady came at six
To get her eve's work done;
And when she reached the executive's room
She'd always find her gone.
The executive always worked past five;
Often till six, and yet,
With checking in and checking out
And moving here and thereabout,
The two had never met.

The cleaning lady always knew
The executive was black,
Just as she was, for several things
Revealed to her that fact.
In the office she'd seen a picture she guessed
Was the executive's family,
Her diploma from Atlanta U,
Dionne's recording, *Déjà vu,*
And a copy of *Ebony.*

And yet, she seemed so unprepared
For that day arranged by fate
When into the office she strolled to find
Its occupant working late.
She stopped as though she'd struck a wall,
And stood rooted like a tree.
To stay or leave, both seemed unwise,
And the seconds which followed as eyes met eyes
Seemed an eternity.

The executive was the first to speak
As she motioned the cleaner to stay.
"Come in," she said, "and do your work.
Hope I'm not in your way."
"No, please. No Ma'am. I wouldn't want
To inconvenience you.
I'll clean another one meantime,
For I can come back anytime,
But that's important work you do."

"And let no one," the executive said,
"Say less of what you do;
For, though you're not behind this desk,
Your work's important too.
And I appreciate your work;
It's a great help to me,
For when I see my office clean,
My mind remains quite clear and keen,
And I work efficiently."

The cleaning lady breathed a sigh
And said, "I'll make it quick.
But I'll be thorough. Don't you fret,
I'll have your office spick.
And that was nice, what you just said
About the work I do.
I clean these rooms until they glow.
And though I'm paid, it's nice to know
That others notice too."

The two engaged in casual talk
As the cleaner did her work.
They spoke of hometowns, and their jobs,
Of families and church.
And the cleaning lady felt the warmth
Of the executive's demeanor;
For she spoke to her with the respect
One would of a youth expect
In deference to an elder.

The executive, too, felt gratified
By the look on the other's face;
For the eyes of the cleaner seemed to say
"You're a credit to our race.
And I could never be more proud
If you were my own daughter."
And so it was that in their way,
The two who met by chance that day,
Did reinforce each other.

They parted to their separate tasks;
Their jobs they couldn't shirk.
But each one found it difficult
To concentrate on work.
They realized they'd shared some time
They wouldn't soon forget;
For each concluded privately
That she, henceforth, would always be
Much richer since they'd met.

The Argument

They argued loud in voices strong,
For each would have his way.
When Otis said that John was wrong,
He heard the other say,
"So Grandpa never hired blacks,
But times were different then.
Should I be punished now for acts
That took place way back when?"

When Otis heard the question posed
His lips curled in a sneer.
With squinted eye and turned-up nose,
He snapped at John, "See here!
You seem to think that bigotry
Has died or gone away,
But racial inequality
Is still alive today."

Instead of backing off, John chose
To liven up the pace.
He glared at Otis, nose to nose,
And told him to his face,
"This new employment that I hear
You call affirmative action
Amounts to nothing more, I fear,
Than reverse discrimination."

But Otis heard it oft before,
The identical attack;
And when he heard it this once more,
He instantly shot back,
"These hiring trends that have you irked
Are justified, because
Voluntary programs never worked,
And affirmative action does."

"Oh sure! It works for you and yours,"
John vehemently said,
"But we're the ones who meet closed doors,
While you guys move ahead.
And yet you have the gall to say
The system holds you back,
When there's no way to lose today
If your skin color's black."

By now, John clearly showed the fire
Of anger held inside.
He saw his chance to vent his ire,
And would not be denied.
He thought since he'd already said
As much as he had done,
He might as well just go ahead
And end what he'd begun.

He snarled, "I know it's legal now
To victimize us whites;
And with the laws supporting you,
You've got us dead to rights.
But answer truly, if you dare
Put truth before your pride,
Do you believe this action's fair,
And morally justified?"

He thought he'd cornered Otis there,
For surely, he'd admit
That in the realm of all that's fair,
These laws just didn't fit.
Anticipating this reply,
John stood in readiness.
But Otis looked him in the eye,
And shouted back, "Hell yes!"

T'was evident that this reply
Took John somewhat aback;
But he recovered soon to hie
Back into the attack.
"I hear you, pal, but ask you this,
Explain it, if you would.
Your rhetoric I wouldn't miss.
I bet your story's good."

"We're at each other's throat right now,"
Came Otis' calm response.
"We're solving nothing with this row;
Each acting like a dunce.
Now I'm prepared to keep my cool,
If you will do the same,
So I can let you hear my point."
And John replied, "I'm game."

"Now, let's imagine," Otis said,
"A two car race we see;
One auto's white, the other's black;
Like milk and ebony,
From north to south their course proceeds
Along I Ninety-five
From Trenton to St. Augustine;
A thousand miles to drive.

"And from the start, the white car speeds
At a good and steady pace,
For not one obstacle impedes
Its progress in this race.
But no such luck befalls the black
As it starts along its way;
For in its path there lies a crack
To cause it some delay.

"And also, lots of shattered glass
To slow it down still more.
And potholes, nails, a dark impasse,
And many a long detour.
And here and there a mire of tar,
And snags of every kind.
It isn't long before this car
Falls very far behind.

"And you and I are named to be
Officials of this run.
And in these roles we're charged to see
The advantage goes to none.
Should we then keep the status quo,
And look the other way
To let the race maintain its flow?"
And John replied, "No way!

"To stay the progress of the black
Can't possibly be right.
It's just as wrong to hold one back
Who happens to be white.
And I'll declare, 'It's wrong,' again,
Just as I did before."
But Otis interrupted then,
"And said, "Wait, John; there's more.

"You're right; there's gross injustice here,
Which we will now correct.
We'll make the road conditions fair;
All obstacles we'll eject.
But with this done, the white we find
Has crossed I Sixty-four,
While the black's two hundred miles behind,
Still north of Baltimore.

"Now, since we took the barriers down
And made the roadways clear,
Should we just let the race go on,
And think that all is fair?
If that's our choice, let's be aware
That we will doom the black
To run this course filled with despair
Of ever bouncing back.

"You see, the past has some effect
On what is happening now.
And there are times we have to check
Its influence, somehow.
You must agree that in this case
The impact is unjust.
So, as the judges of this race,
Correct it then, we must.

"Now, I suggest whatever's right
Is what we ought to do.
We'll let the black catch up the white
Before the contest's through.
Then in the stretch both cars can move
On an equitable base.
And only then can we conclude
We've a fair, unbiased race.

"We shouldn't think of holding back
The white car in its place.
Instead, we should assist the black
By speeding up its pace.
To stand a chance to overcome
The gap the past has left,
The black car must accelerate,
And thus close up that cleft."

"I think I see the parallel
You're trying to draw," said John,
"Between employing personnel
And the motor run."
"You're right," said Otis, "It's the same
In the employment scene.
Though legislation's changed the game,
The gap remains between.

"But we must never dare suggest
Denying jobs to whites
In order to overcome the past.
Such action isn't right.
We should increase the applicant flow
Of blacks who seek careers.
The more the hiring sources grow,
The more the chance of hires.

"So if we use white agencies,
And colleges, and press
To generate white applicants,
For blacks, should we do less?
No! We must use the black press too,
And any other source,
Like black schools, which will help us to
Increase the black workforce.

"We should examine practices
That adversely affect
Some human beings because of race.
Such acts we must correct.
Like letting all white working crews
Refer their kin and friends.
Some companies employ this ruse
To keep their hiring trends.

"And companies who've changed their ways
May see no blacks apply.
Recalling former hurtful days,
They'll think they needn't try.
So firms must go and seek them out
And let them know they're welcome,
And turn that widening gap about.
Now that's affirmative action.

"So when you ask do I believe
This kind of action's fair,
'Yes! Surely as I live and breathe!'
Is all you're going to hear.
Not only do I think it's fair,
And bolstered in our courts,
But I aver with all my might,
'Affirmative action works!'"

Said John, "Your colorful defense
Of things I've often fought,
Admittedly, shows common sense,
And leaves me food for thought.
I'll mull it over for a while,
And then get back to you."
But Otis merely forced a smile.
T'was over, and he knew.

All by Themselves

I see them everywhere now,
These black executives.
They're in the media,
In sports and business.
They broadcast, coach, consult,
Manage corporations, plants, and departments.
Most impress me.
Some seem full of their own importance.
But overall, I'm pleased to see them.

But then I hear some speak.
And their words cut deep
As I hear them express so forcefully
Their heartfelt contempt
For affirmative action.
They're opposed, they claim,
Because they want others to know,
And they want to feel within themselves,
That their successes were not due
To boosts received from legislation
Relevant to their color.
They need to be able to proclaim
That their achievements
Were due to their talents and efforts alone.
They did it all by themselves.

All by themselves?
The thought makes my head spin.
Was it an overnight change
From the days of flaunted discrimination
To these days of equal opportunity?
Were there no decades of transition?
No pioneers to take the brunt of hostility
For being among the first to force a breach?
No picketing?
No boycotts?
No landmark court decisions?
Did not the threat of losing government contracts
Affect employment practices?
Was having to demonstrate affirmative action
Of no coercive value?
Did they really succeed all by themselves?

As I ponder their outrageous claim,
I am reminded to think kindly of the ones
Who acknowledge the efforts of others.
And I give thanks
For the statutes, sacrifices, and efforts,
Which have been so successful,
They enable many who have benefited
To now oppose them.
After all, they did it all by themselves
Yeah! Right!